AF579945

Porch Stories

by Stefanie Congdon

ISBN: 979-8-9948918-1-0

Second Edition

For Grace—
the OG MCD bum

What Is This Place?

Mackinac Island sits in the Straits of Mackinac, between Michigan's Upper and Lower Peninsulas. More than eighty percent of the island is preserved as Michigan State Park, protecting its limestone bluffs, wooded trails, and historic landmarks. Cars have been prohibited since 1898, leaving horses and bicycles to carry everything from groceries to wedding guests.

Today, Mackinac is part historic landmark and part living community. In summer, the docks fill with ferries and crowds. In winter, snowmobiles replace bikes and the island quiets into something smaller and more intimate.

For eight years, I lived and worked on the island. I managed The Inn at Stonecliffe, the great old mansion set high above the Straits. This was the Stonecliffe before its forty-million-dollar restoration and rebirth as a humanitarian hotel donating profits to causes worldwide. My Stonecliffe was imperfect and a little creaky, but alive with people, conversations, and the small moments that made it feel like home.

I always found my way back to the front porch of the Mansion. No matter how busy the day, no matter how many details waited inside, I'd slip outside for a few minutes, drawn by the steady clip-clop of hooves in the drive. The porch was my reset, my favorite place to be. From there, I could watch the flow of the estate. Porters lifting bags with ease, horses stamping as they waited for the next run, guests stepping into the sunshine with that wide-eyed look only Mackinac Island seems to inspire.

The porch itself was its own world. Old red brick stretched underfoot, the turret stood watch beside the steps, and flowers framed the lawn. A red maple stood against the kitchen windows, and the lilac tree, blooming only briefly each spring, somehow lingers in my memory as if it flowered all season.

It was also where the best conversations happened. Guests arrived from every corner of the country and sometimes the world. I loved to ask where they were from, what had brought them to Mackinac, how they had spent their day. Their answers became a map of island experiences. A bike ride around the shore, a picnic at Arch Rock, a swim in the pool, a visit to a favorite shop, or a stop for fudge. Every conversation carried a spark of discovery. And inevitably, the questions circled back to me. "What do you do all winter? Do children really go to school here? Is it haunted?"

My porters could have repeated the answers word for word. They heard them daily. I never minded. I loved answering, because it meant sharing a little piece of island life. Sometimes it was a story about Mackinac winters, sometimes about my daughter at the tiny island school, who was learning to fly airplanes, or a hint of mystery from the Mansion's long history. Pieces of information used to kill time until the next carriage arrived.

That history was part of the porch, too. Stonecliffe was built in 1904 by Michael Cudahy and designed by Chicago architect Frederick Perkins, who also designed the Governor's Summer Residence. Later, the Hert family owned the estate. Sallie Hert herself was a nationally known political leader who fought for women's suffrage. Over the decades, the property passed through many hands, surviving reinventions that ranged from summer retreat to ski hill experiment. By the time I came along, Stonecliffe had already lived many lives.

Those porch conversations became a ritual, the part of the day that reminded me why I loved this life. A view of the Straits, the shuffle of horses, a question asked, a story shared. And always, a history that seemed to live right there in the open air. Every exchange reminded me that Mackinac was more than a place to live and work. It was a story unfolding, one guest at a time.

The Mansion

The Mansion had sixteen rooms, each with its own personality. I could tell stories about every one of them, and often did. But a few always stood out, for better or worse.

Most days, someone would wander into the Mansion, wide-eyed and bewildered. They'd be biking the island, find their way up the hill, and suddenly, there it was. A sprawling estate they had never heard of. I must have given hundreds of tours that way, pointing out the original woodwork in the lobby, the cherubs on the fireplace in the dining room, and the little coffin-like hiding storage spaces tucked beneath the benches.

To feel the history, you only had to step inside the Mansion itself. The entryway felt both grand and intimate. Dark Edwardian wood framed every corner, polished by time. Straight ahead, a set of doors led into the restaurant. To the left, the bar. To the right, the front desk, tucked into a corner. The woodwork gave the whole space a gravity that reminded you the Mansion had stood there for more than a century.

You climbed a grand set of stairs, watched by a soldier believed to have been painted by the artist Louis Betts.

The Mackinac Room was the jewel of the house. It had four-poster bed, a built-in vanity, and windows looking out toward the Straits and the Mackinac Bridge. Many brides sat at that vanity for her wedding portraits, framed by the same light that once belonged to Mrs. Cudahy herself.

Down the hall was Mr. Cudahy's room, simply called the Cudahy Room. Its layout was simple, and the view unmatched with two full walls of windows, the most spectacular in the Mansion. Together, the two rooms held the original heartbeat of the estate. A husband and wife, looking out on the Straits of Mackinac from their separate corners of the house.

The Islander room stood apart from the other third-floor rooms. Long before it was a guest room, it had been the family theater. The high window once sat behind the stage. I imagined evenings of piano, gramophone, and laughter that must have carried down the stairs. Later, it became a guest room with two queen beds, but you could still sense its past. A reminder of the Mansion's life before screens, when entertainment meant gathering together in one room.

Then there was Maplewood, the smallest room in the building. It had everything it needed: a bed, a window, a door that closed, and not much more. Guests sometimes laughed when they first walked in, surprised by its scale, but Maplewood suited those who spent their days exploring the island. Every mansion needs an underdog, and this was ours.

But the feature everyone asked about was the turret. From the first day I saw it, it was my favorite part of the Mansion. Its spiral staircase stitched the building together, running from the basement to the third floor. The basement doors led to storage spaces and some employee housing. On the first floor, the turret opened into the kitchen, then rose through the Straits Room and guest hallways, ending with the little Maplewood room on the third floor. It was as much a showpiece as it was the backbone of our operation.

The turret overlooked the front grounds, where carriages came and went. From its windows, you could watch the rhythm of arrivals and departures, wheels crunching over the drive. My favorite snapshot is from the screened turret window on the second floor, looking down toward the porch. Horses lined up, luggage carts rolling, guests arriving, staff falling into step. From above, it looked effortless, though I knew how much work it took to keep things moving as they should.

The turret had its secrets, too. One year, a construction crew pulled a tube sock out of the wall. It had been crammed in, plastered over, and sealed until that day. Why? To plug a hole? A prank? A time capsule? No one could say. It was absurd and charming all at once, like the turret itself. A little mysterious, and utterly essential.

Not all the surprises were bricks or beams. Sometimes the Mansion offered up pieces of its own history. A neighbor once biked over with six stained-glass panels she had found in her basement, wrapped in newspapers and tied with twine. They were from the days when Stonecliffe was part of a ski resort. The glass showed slalom skiers, cross-country tracks, and the initials MH, short for Mount Humbard. We learned they had once been installed in the front windows at The Woods, the old playhouse now run as a restaurant by the Grand Hotel.

Other relics were downright charming. In a closet, we found a painting of someone wearing a red hat. I studied it often, wondering who the sitter was, who the artist was, and how it had come to live in a closet at Stonecliffe. The lore was that it should never leave the

Mansion, or bad luck would follow. After a season of sewage woes, and heading into 2020, I decided to flip the curse on its head. We hung the red hat portrait front and center in the bar of the Cudahy Chophouse, a symbol that better things were ahead.

And you can't miss the Portico. It stretched along the west side of the Mansion, framing the Mackinac Bridge in the distance. Breakfast on the Portico was one of our quiet luxuries, a perfect way to start the day before the island woke up. At night, it transformed. You'd find guests sipping cocktails, honeymooners clinking glasses, and the bridge lights flickering in the dark. The sunsets there were spectacular, the sky on fire, water catching every shade.

Sixteen rooms, each with its own story. Some glamorous, some humble. To guests, they were more than just places to stay. Each had its loyalists, the ones who saved up year after year to return to the same room. For some, it was an anniversary tradition. For others, a birthday wish or a family reunion. To me, they were a cast of characters, each one shaping the life inside the Mansion.

The Summer House

If the turret was the Mansion's artery, then the basement of the Summer House was its heartbeat. Guest laundry was found down there, vending machines, the bride's "get-ready" room, and the heart of the house, our housekeeping headquarters. The admin offices, storage rooms, and even a one bedroom manager's apartment kept the place alive year-round. In the off-season, reservations were taken from that very basement. It was our connection to the outside world when our co-workers were often the only people we saw all day.

Upstairs, the vibe shifted. The Summer House was newer, practical, and cottage-like. The walls came in shades of green, beige, yellow, or, my favorite, blue. Families loved it for the two-bedroom suites. Bridal parties booked it for the extra bathrooms, and every room came with a sofa bed for kids or extra guests. Each unit had a mini-fridge, a microwave, a wet bar and dishes. Most importantly, the Summer House had air conditioning. That alone was the deciding factor for many guests. These days, the Mansion has air conditioning too, thanks to the forty-million-dollar renovation.

Most Summer House rooms came with balconies facing the treeline and, if you were lucky, the Straits of Mackinac. My favorite was Room 2312. With two balconies, its view outshone even some of the Mansion's storied rooms. You could step outside in either direction and watch the horizon unfold, a quieter, more sensible kind of luxury.

That was the Summer House. The practical side of the hotel. Book the Summerhouse if you wanted comfort, space to unwind, and modern amenities. Choose the Mansion if you wanted history, quirks, and charm. Together, the two buildings made Stonecliffe what it was. A hotel that could hold both stories at once.

For all its practicality, the Summer House still carried the stamp of Mackinac. There might have been fridges and air conditioning inside, but outside it was bikes parked by the door and horse taxis dropping you off. Modern comfort, lived on island terms.

The Grounds

Spring was all about color. Tulips, daffodils, crocuses, hyacinths, pansies and peonies. We were surrounded by them all. After a gray, wind-battered winter, those pops of color meant everything. Guests noticed. The staff noticed. I noticed.

The showpiece was a patch we called Lilac Island with purples, blues and whites radiating in the middle of the yard. We tucked a little seating area inside the lilac trees so guests could sit surrounded by fragrant blooms.

Hydrangeas circled the pool, another shot of color framing the view.

By summer, the pool itself turned into a postcard. Brilliant blue water set against a brand-new deck, rows of blue umbrellas, and lounge chairs lined up to face the Straits. From the pool, you could see the bridge gleaming in the distance. The Portico, our grand back porch, looked out on it all, with lawn seating fanned out below. Weddings, dinners, and parties spilled into the yard like it was an outdoor ballroom.

Tucked into the side yard was the Grotto, shaded and quiet, a little world of its own. An old stone fountain sat there, trickling water, its basin filled with moss and lily pads. Guests often stumbled on it by accident, surprised to find such a secret pocket of green so close to the bustle of the Portico.

In the fall, corn stalks, pumpkins, and mums lined the walkways, but nothing compared to the beautiful red maple in front of the Mansion by the kitchen window. It flamed brighter than anything else on the property, and it was always my favorite tree. Guests posed under it without even realizing it was hiding the kitchen windows.

Winter made the yard almost unrecognizable. The Mansion stood bare, the lawn covered in snow. The roads weren't plowed, just packed down enough that a fire truck could get through if needed. We kept the hydrants shoveled out, a job no one ever fought to claim. One local man groomed a cross-country ski track right through the yard with his snowmobile, neat parallel lines curving across the white. It gave the place a touch of beauty months when the Mansion looked lonely and still.

Beyond the formal lawn, the path led through what remained of the old apple orchard. In its prime, it must have been a place of harvest, but in my years, it was more of a passageway with gnarled trees framing the path toward Sunset Rock. It was an in-between place, a threshold, carrying you from the clipped grounds of the estate to the wild edge of the island where the sun met the water.

From the front yard, you had the activity. The carriages pulling in, bikes lined up, the laughter of guests coming and going across the expansive lawn. It was the social side of the estate, always in motion. Step around back and it shifted completely. The Straits of Mackinac stretched wide, the bridge cutting across the horizon, sunsets setting the water on fire. It was one of the best views on the island, and it belonged to the Mansion's backyard.

Do You Guys Do Weddings?

I'll never forget my very first wedding at Stonecliffe. In the excitement of it all, I managed to peek my head right into the couple's arrival photo, smiling from the Mansion window behind them. Maybe I've been photoshopped out by now. Or maybe I'm still hanging over their fireplace, watching as their family grows.

That was the beginning of what became a part of our routine. Weddings were common, sometimes as many as 65 per season. A Friday arrival was the most familiar pattern. Guests and family would tumble up to the porch, arms full of garment bags and gift bags, their laughter spilling into the lobby. We'd greet everyone, making sure they knew where to be and when. Then they set off for a rehearsal dinner someplace wonderful. Perhaps The Woods, tucked in the forest with its Bavarian charm, or the Pink Pony downtown, buzzing with colorful lake views.

By Saturday morning, the familiar faces were back, the house alive with anticipation. Bridesmaids filled the little "get ready" room beside my office, a flurry of curling irons, makeup brushes, and dresses swishing past the doorway. Finger sandwiches and mimosas steadied the nerves, and someone inevitably needed scissors. Our sales manager, genius that she was, always had a kit ready with safety pins, hairspray, and even a spare pair of nylons. She was a quiet hero, saving many a morning.

Ceremonies could unfold in many places. On the back lawn overlooking the Straits, on the front lawn with the Mansion rising in view, or tucked into the Grotto. The Grotto was always my favorite. Sometimes it was dressed up with flowers and lanterns, and once I saw it transformed with hundreds of glowing orbs strung from the trees. But most often, it didn't need a thing. The fountain trickled softly, the woods wrapped close, and the whole place felt private, sacred, and timeless. If I were ever to marry on Mackinac, I'd choose the Grotto without hesitation.

From there, the magic unfolded. Cocktail hour floated across the lawn with trays of butler-passed hors d'oeuvres. Mini quiches, tiny beef Wellingtons, crisp crab Rangoons, and little bites that disappeared in a single taste. Guests mingled and laughed while the last-minute touches fell into place.

I always loved those little details that made the night sparkle. Lighting the candles, dimming the lights, giving the DJ a thumbs-up, high-fiving the sales manager and banquet manager for pulling off another miracle, and thanking the kitchen staff.

Dinner followed, each course prepared by the chef and cooked right on-site in the Stonecliffe kitchen. Plates left the pass steaming and perfect, carrying the same care and craft as the celebration itself.

And then, of course, the cake. Over the years, I tasted more bites than I could ever count. Cakes balanced in bike baskets, cakes decorated with tiny sugar ladybugs hiding in the frosting, cakes that arrived like little works of art. Each one was its own sweet ending, a final note to a day already full of love.

After dinner, the real party began. The first notes of the daddy-daughter dance always caught me off guard. Tender and timeless, it got me every single time. From there, the DJ spun tunes, filling the floor with energy. The party carried on in full swing, laughter and music spilling out into the night. Sometimes the wedding guests would even try to pull us out onto the dance floor, blurring the line between host and celebrant.

The dancing wrapped at ten, the sky painting itself in brilliant color for a sunset send-off. But the night was young. We'd load wedding guests into carriages, sending them off for a few more hours of music and merriment downtown, where Mackinac Island after dark worked its own kind of magic.

In the morning, it was always fun to see the same faces I had poured red wine for the night before. I'd watched their choreographed entrances, I'd heard their speeches, and I might even have been the one to serve their wedding cake. By then, we'd shared a weekend together, and it always felt personal when they came back to the front porch with luggage in tow, smiling and tired, on their way to the ferry.

Upon departure, we were sometimes rewarded with hugs, goodbyes, and promises to return for their anniversary. Many did, coming back each year, sometimes with babies in tow. Stonecliffe had become part of their family tradition, and I loved seeing their families grow.

Wedding advice I'd offer? Use local vendors whenever possible. Getting equipment to and from the hotel is challenging, and for someone unfamiliar with the island, it can be daunting. I saw many DJs sweating bullets on the front porch, waiting for speakers and cables to arrive only minutes before the ceremony began.

Local photographers are worth every penny. They already know the best lighting, the hidden corners of the island, how long it takes to get from place to place, and where to stop when the backdrop will be perfect. Some of my favorite wedding moments happened after the ceremony, when the bride and groom climbed into a carriage for a private ride around the island while the photographers followed behind on bicycles, stopping them along the way for portraits at overlooks, hedges, and quiet little pockets a non-local photographer might not know about.

Local florists and cake designers understood island logistics too. Flowers wilt faster than people expect in July heat, cakes travel by ferry and carriage, and timing matters for everything. The vendors who worked here regularly knew how to adapt when weather, ferry schedules, or island timing threw little surprises their way.

So when guests asked if we really did weddings here, I could only smile and say yes. *Magical ones.*

What Should We Do Today?

Every day the question found me on the porch.

"What should we do today?"

I always stuck to my favorites, tried and true. The things I knew would never disappoint.

First, take a carriage tour at least once. Mackinac Island Carriage Tours starts downtown, with smaller wagons that pull you up the Grand Hill to the Carriage Museum and Stables. From there, the big three-horse teams take over, carrying you past the cemeteries, Skull Cave, Arch Rock, and all the sights you'll want to revisit later. It's the easiest way to see the island if you're short on time or can't do the hills yourself. My advice was always to take a tour once to get the lay of the land Then next time, rent a bike and find those places on your own.

If they had little kids, I'd send them to one of the butterfly houses on the island, often pointing them toward the one tucked behind St. Anne's Church. It's bright and magical and just the right size for the short attention spans.

Bored teens? Bistro on the Greens at Mission Point Resort. Let them play a round on the putting course, grab lunch, and burn off some of that restless energy.

Older adults, or anyone who needed a slower pace? I'd recommend a personal carriage tour. Those drivers could pick you up right in front of Stonecliffe and take you wherever you wanted to go.

And if you were the type who just wanted to relax, I'd suggest the pool. From the deck, you could float or lounge and still see the Straits of Mackinac stretched out beside you, the bridge rising like a gateway on the horizon. Sometimes the best way to see Mackinac was to stop moving altogether.

Rent a bike. Or bring your own. The island is best explored on two wheels.

Go left where you'd normally go right. Wander into neighborhoods with beautiful old houses, porches sagging with history. Stop in the cemeteries and pay your respects. Huff your way up to Fort Holmes, the highest point on the island, and look out over it all.

Bike the perimeter of the island if you've got the time. It is one of my favorite memories of visiting with my daughter and nephew years before working there was even a spark. Stop at every mile marker for a selfie. Ride British Landing Road and pause at the old battleground sites. Stop at Cannonball for deep-fried pickles, an island tradition. Explore Brown's Brook, where the water gurgles through a quiet cut in the rocks. Skip stones at Windermere Point and watch the ripples spread out toward the bridge.

Take your time, and remember how easy it is to get to Mackinac Island. You'll be back. Don't try to tackle it all in one trip.

If you really want to feel like you've uncovered something, hunt down Crack in the Island. It's not much to look at, just a split in the limestone. But finding it makes you feel like you've strayed far off the beaten path and stumbled onto something secret and important.

And whatever you do, don't miss the sunset. From the Portico and back lawn at Stonecliffe, it's a show all its own. Or you could venture through the yard to Sunset Rock, and see the beautiful view of the Mackinac Bridge with tiny cars and trucks inching their way north or south.

For the perfect weekend, add a night out. Put on something fancy and head to the Grand Hotel. Cocktails, jazz, and the kind of atmosphere that makes you feel like you've stepped into another era. Before or after, linger at one of the downtown bars, taking in the live music, everywhere.

If you find yourself downtown late at night, grab a "Pub Sub" from Horns. You won't find it on their menu, but the bartenders will lead you in the right direction.

If you take only one piece of advice from me, make it this.

Stay Sunday night.

Let the rush of the weekend slip away with the departing ferries. Walk down Main Street when it's quiet, or sit on the porch and hear the island breathe again.

Monday morning, when the sun rises over a half-empty dock, you will feel like the smartest person alive when you board the ferry without waiting in a long line.

What Do You Do All Winter?

It was the question I heard more than any other, asked on the porch in summer by wide-eyed guests who couldn't imagine Mackinac without fudge shops and ferries. They'd tilt their heads, half curious, half skeptical, and say, "But what do you *do* all winter?"

The short answer came first. Winter was for renovation. It was the season of capital projects. Painting, plumbing, repairs and improvements that couldn't be tackled in the rush of summer. While the island seemed to sleep under snow, island businesses and inns were quietly being readied for another season. That was my job, and it always felt like the most practical reply.

But the longer answer was harder to explain.

Winter on Mackinac was another world. When the last passenger ferry left in late October, the island seemed to exhale. Streets went quiet, shutters closed, and horses were sent to pasture on the mainland. Snowmobiles replaced bikes, their engines roaring down the same paths that only weeks before were crowded with carriages and tourists. The air turned sharp, the lake froze hard, and silence spread across the island like a blanket.

Some days were lonely, the kind where you could walk down Main Street and not see another soul. But that same stillness made the smallest sparks of community glow brighter. A hockey game under the streetlights, a chili cook-off at the VI, a Christmas bazaar that filled the community center with warmth and laughter.

Life slowed, but it didn't stop. We bundled into snow gear for errands, hauled groceries by snowmobile, and measured the weeks by traditions and gatherings. My daughter trudged off to the little school, her world as normal as any child's. My days were built of snowdrifts and crackling fires, long evenings with books, and the joy when friends braved the Straits to visit.

So what did we do all winter? We worked, we adapted, and we found ways to make it our own. We painted and hammered, baked and laughed, dragged Christmas trees home by snowmobile, roasted hot dogs in the snow, and filled quiet nights with stories. The island never disappeared in winter. It just revealed another side of itself. A side that many never experience.

Christmas Bazaar

The Christmas Bazaar was a Mackinac tradition. Every December, the island gathered for a fundraiser that supported the Mackinac Island Medical Center and local churches. The community center overflowed with tables piled high for the thrift sale, a mix of castoffs, hand-me-downs, and treasures you didn't know you needed until you saw them. Snow piled up outside, but inside it was warm and crowded, everyone rubbing shoulders and laughing as they dug through bins of scarves, knickknacks, and holiday decorations.

I contributed in the way I knew how. I baked. Loaves of bread, plates of cookies, even dog treats, each wrapped in neat little baggies with holiday ribbons. My daughter Grace delivered the treats on her snowmobile, stacking them neatly on the table before slipping out.

The bazaar wasn't just about baked goods and bargains. It spilled into downtown, where shops and bars opened their doors for holiday shopping. Tourists might trickle in, but it was mostly a locals' thing. Islanders and cottagers, year-round staff bundled in scarves and hats, cocoa in some hands, whiskey in others. Snowflakes dusted the windows as people wandered from storefront to storefront.

We got our wreaths from the bazaar, but the Christmas trees came from a beautiful and weathered old barn on the corner of Cadotte and Market Streets. It was an honor system. You picked your tree and drove it home on the back of your snowmobile, or in your bike basket, depending on the weather and your strength, and paid later. Some years, a tree stood on the front steps of the Mansion. Other years, just a wreath. But we did what we could to give it some love, even if it was only seen by a select few.

One year, we even set up a tree in the Grotto, a quiet secret, peeking out from a blanket of snow for whoever might find it.

The highlight of the Christmas Bazaar was the tree lighting, right in the middle of Main Street. We'd gather around in the crisp air, huddled close as the carols started. The mayor, the same mayor Mackinac Island had trusted for more than fifty years, would give a wave and the big tree blazed to life. For a moment, it was pure magic, the whole island glowing in the middle of winter.

There was also hockey. Not the polished, televised kind, but a street game played right on Main Street. They call it Bynoe hockey, after the man who loves the game most.

Bynoe is part of the fabric of Mackinac, and his team always wins. Even if the score said otherwise, everyone agreed. Bynoe's team won. The fire chief roasted hot dogs for the crowd, and music blared from loudspeakers as mittened hands clutched ketchup-streaked buns while the snow came down.

The Christmas Bazaar was uniquely ours. Charity and chaos, magic and mischief. Hot dogs in the snow, the glow of the downtown tree, and Bynoe's unstoppable hockey team. Friends haggling over necklaces, locals slipping into shops for gifts, and me quietly sending loaves of bread out into the crowd. Every year, it reminded me that even in the dead of winter, Mackinac Island could still come alive.

The Walk

Every fall, talk would begin about the Christmas Walk, which was a progressive dinner. It was a neighborhood tradition in the Stonecliffe and Sunset Forest neighborhoods. By December, everything would be arranged. Hosts lined up, invitations hand-delivered, and always a homemade treat tucked inside.

The Walk was simple. Appetizers at one house, a hearty dish at another, and dessert at the last stop. I volunteered to host dessert two years in a row.

The catch? Dessert would be in the closed-up Mansion with no plumbing. The basement apartment had a working bathroom, but that meant a trip down the turret stairs to use it. Nobody minded. These were island friends, summer neighbors turned winter family.

What mattered was the glow. For the first time in years, the Mansion sparkled with Christmas cheer. With the help of neighbors, we strung lights until every corner twinkled. My dog, Cooper, tore happily around the Mansion as we worked, soaked and shivering, but delighted by the bustle, as if he were part of the celebration too.

I set out a hot cocoa bar, complete with every topping I could think of. Whipped cream, candy canes, marshmallows, and even sprinkles. A slow cooker with steaming glühwein scented the air with cloves and cinnamon. On the table, I laid out miniature desserts, including pecan pies, carrot cakes, cheesecakes, and Christmas cookies. It was like a little bakery exploded into the room. Soft, jazzy Christmas music floated from the speakers, the fireplace roared, and skewers waited for anyone who wanted to roast a marshmallow over the flames. Cooper greeted each guest at the door, wagging his tail as if they'd all come just to see him.

The neighborhood showed up, helmets lined by the door, coats stacked high on chairs. Laughter filled the halls, and for a rare wintertime evening, the Mansion felt alive again.

Chili Cook-Off

The Village Inn (back then we all just called it the VI) was one of two winter hubs, the other being the Mustang. Trivia nights, game nights, football games, or just a drink for the sake of camaraderie, that's where we gathered. By February, tourists had mostly disappeared, but the VI was alive with locals, and one of the highlights of the season was the annual chili cook-off.

Getting the ingredients wasn't simple. That winter, I placed a special order with a grocery store in St. Ignace. They packed it up, drove it to the airport, and the tiny plane flew it across the Straits. All I had to do was hop on our trusty snowmobile and swing by the airport to pick it up, grateful for the errand and that I didn't have to fly over myself that day.

Finally, I could cook. I sliced and diced to music in my kitchen, making the chili in small batches. Nothing tastes as good in bulk as it does in a small pot. I made five batches that day. I set each pot out in the snow outside my front door to chill. I poured the thick mixture into borrowed Cambros, steam rising into the cold air against the backdrop of the frozen Straits.

Inside, my fireplace smoked sweetly, and the whole place smelled of bacon and spice.

“Bacon in chili? That’s cheating,” someone once said. Maybe. But it was delicious.

When it was time, I loaded all five Cambros into the utility trailer that dragged behind the snowmobile. The ride to town was slow and careful, every bump threatening to jostle the cargo. I nodded helmet to helmet at others on the trail, all of us newly compliant with the police chief’s new law. For my first winter, we rode bare-headed, but now helmets were mandatory.

The VI was packed, heat and laughter spilling out the doors. The winter vestibule was lined with helmets and snow suits. Gear piled high as people shook off the cold before stepping inside. Front and center in the room stood the chili tables, each offering something different.

I struck up a conversation with a couple who had just returned from traveling around the world. They were new to me then, but would become part of my circle in the winters to come. That’s how Mackinac worked. Friendships often started over something as simple as a shared meal in the middle of a long, cold season.

I was happy and hopeful that day, proud to set my hearty chili among the rest. It didn’t win, but participating felt like winning to me, and that was enough.

Do You Go on the Ice Bridge?

No. The answer is an absolute no.

The ice bridge is a frozen stretch between St. Ignace and Mackinac Island that forms in the coldest winters. When conditions allowed, brave souls marked the "road" with discarded Christmas trees. Some winters it was a full-blown highway. Construction crews hauling tools on sleds pulled behind snowmobiles, people saving on flight costs, friends zipping over for lunch or a manicure.

Snowmobiles race, skiers glide, fat-tire bikes wobble across, and sometime, even walkers appear.

It looks romantic, a secret road across the Straits. But it's unpredictable and deadly if you misjudge.

The ice cannot be trusted. One bitter six-degree day, my daughter and her dad took snowmobiles out near British Landing for photos. Even close to shore, on what looked like solid ice, she went through. She shot her arms up, phone safe as was a teenager's priority, scrambled out, and sped home, legs burning and tingling with cold. We stripped her wet clothes, got her warmed up, sat her next to the fire, and she was fine. But from then on, I stopped trusting the ice.

Some veterans know what they're doing. I've seen their daring runs. But Mackinac's tiny fire and rescue crews and the U.S. Coast Guard shouldn't have to risk lives for a novice's adventure, or so they can tick an item off a bucket list. So no. I don't recommend the ice bridge. The lake doesn't care how confident you are.

What's Your Favorite Place on the Island?

That was always a hard question to answer, because it depended on the day, the season, and what kind of quiet I was looking for.

If I had only an hour to myself, I'd head straight to Sunset Rock. It's close to the Mansion, just far enough for a quick escape, and the view never failed me. The Straits stretched wide, the Mackinac Bridge in the distance, and if I timed it right, sunset.

If I wanted real solitude, I'd climb to Fort Holmes, with a pause at Point Lookout on the way up. But the true summit is Fort Holmes, the island's highest point. There is a cool fort up there, so you can get your history fix while taking in breathtaking views. It's a little off the beaten path and not an easy pedal up, which means it's rarely crowded.

And when guests asked me about restaurants, I often started closer to home. Our own restaurant at Stonecliffe. And I always recommended the Pink Pony, specifically their patio, and a rumrunner. Everyone needs to feel that wild, colorful energy at least once in their life.

After a long day, though, I sometimes just wanted to sit somewhere with a glass in my hand and people around me. I'd head to Bistro on the Greens at Mission Point. It sat right in the middle of an eighteen-hole putting course, surrounded by bubbling brooks and colorful blooms. From there, the view stretched out over the lake, and was one of my favorite spots on the island.

For dinner, if I really wanted to indulge, I'd go to The Woods. Their short ribs alone were reason enough. Rich and tender, the kind of plate you lingered over. After dinner, I always loved a round of duckpin bowling, imagining what this place must have been like back when it served as a playhouse for the children of the Stonecliffe mansion.

For something simpler, there was the Chuckwagon Restaurant downtown. It's a classic diner, great for breakfast or a burger when you simply need fuel without fuss.

But if I really wanted to treat myself? A night out at the Grand Hotel. Getting dressed up, sitting down to a five-course meal with wines chosen by the sommelier, and closing the evening with live jazz and dancing in their historic ballroom. It was pure island magic, always the highlight of my season. Highly recommend.

And when they asked if I ever got tired of the fudge? Not once. The smell drifted down Main Street before you even reached the shops. People pressed their noses to the glass, watching the fudge fold on the marble tables. Everyone had a favorite.

So, my favorite place? I could never choose just one. Each season, each corner of the island had its own claim on me.

What Is It Like Raising Kids Here?

I can't speak for raising a child on Mackinac Island from the start, since Grace was twelve when we arrived. But I can tell you what it was like to parent a teenager there, in a place where the island itself shaped her every day.

Grace definitely had more freedom on Mackinac Island than kids on the mainland. I never worried about her getting behind the wheel with a brand-new driver's license, or the darker fears that haunt parents elsewhere. Her days always included a bike ride in summer or a snowmobile ride in winter, no matter the weather. Even in storms. She had the kind of independence most teenagers only dream about. But it wasn't freedom without limits.

On Mackinac, all eyes were on you. I'd get texts from friends: "Just saw your kid at Ryba's fudge shop," or "She's on her way up the hill."

At home, she had chores like any other kid, and on Thursdays, she cooked dinner for us. She didn't just cook. She planned the meal, biked to Doud's for ingredients and carried them back in her bike basket. Cooking was something we shared. Some nights we threw meals together side by side, making the most of what we had in the fridge. Of course, there were also the busy evenings when dinner was nothing more than cold chicken over the kitchen sink, but even then, it worked for us.

Grace also helped out at Stonecliffe. She pulled weeds, cleaned up after horses, worked breakfast shifts and banquets, whatever was needed. It wasn't glamorous, but it was life on Mackinac, where everyone pitched in.

Outside of chores and work, the island had its own kind of teenage social life. There were game nights, trivia nights, and teen nights that gave them something to do when boredom set in. They'd play flashlight tag in the woods, army-crawling through the underbrush until someone inevitably ended up with poison ivy. A teenager with poison ivy is no party, and there was no laughing going on when it was her turn.

Sometimes Grace would join me on the front porch at Stonecliffe, chatting with guests as they lingered near the front door, most likely waiting for a taxi. She had a natural way of making conversation, asking where people were from or listening to their stories about how they'd spent time on the island. For me, those evenings felt like a quiet gift. I would be caught up in the rhythm of hospitality, but then I'd glance over and see Grace laughing with someone about their bike ride or offering directions to one place or another. It reminded me that she wasn't only my daughter. She was also part of this place, and the island was shaping her in ways the mainland could not.

On an island that small, news traveled fast. Every teenage misstep felt amplified, which must have been difficult. Grace carried herself through those years with more steadiness than I had at her age, and I was proud of her for that.

But what really defined Grace's island years was her obsession with aviation. She spent long hours at the airport, photographing landings and takeoffs, riding her bike down the runway like she owned it. She was hired on as a teenager, doing odd jobs that kept her close to the planes. The pilots encouraged her, handed her books, and cheered her on. Some even stood beside me at the fence as I watched her takeoffs and landings, knowing how much pride and fear were tangled in my chest.

Grace flew before she drove. While other kids her age studied for driver's tests, she was logging hours in the cockpit. She saved every dollar she earned for flight lessons, working toward that horizon line one paycheck at a time. When she flew her first solo flight off of Mackinac Island, I knew it was more than just a hobby. She wasn't just a teenager passing time. She was hooked.

That's what it was like for me to raise a kid here. A mix of freedom and responsibility, community and closeness, and a daughter who found her place in the sky.

What Is School Like Here?

Guests asked me that question often, as if they couldn't imagine what a school could look like with no cars, no mainland commute, no mall nearby. The answer was simple. It was like any other school, just smaller.

During Grace's time, there were around seventy-two kids, kindergarten through twelfth grade, all under one roof. A single hallway ran the length of the building, littles on one end, older kids on the other. The lockers were dented and ordinary, but they had snowmobile helmet cubbies perched above them instead of locks. The whole place smelled like every school you've ever been in, that unmistakable mix of pencil shavings, sneakers, and cafeteria air.

Teachers wore more hats than most. Some years, classes doubled up, or rotated from year by year. By the time a student graduated, they'd had what they needed. Maybe not in perfect order, but covered all the same. There wasn't a huge selection of electives the way mainland schools had them. Just the basics with some online options, taught by the same handful of teachers year after year. For some kids, it worked fine. For others, like Grace, it was harder. Struggling with math is one thing. Struggling with the same math teacher five years in a row is another.

Her teachers sometimes caught her looking up aviation information during class, lost in another world while algebra dragged on. It wasn't that she didn't care about learning; she just cared about flying more. By the time she graduated, she knew an astonishing amount about airplanes for someone her age. The school couldn't always feed that hunger, but it didn't snuff it out either.

Social life was scaled down, too. There weren't many school dances in the gym, but there were teen nights in the basement of a local church.

In a school that size, there wasn't much separation. Older and younger kids passed each other daily, all ages mixing in the hallway. When there was a concert, a basketball game, or a banquet, the whole island came. It wasn't just the school's event. It belonged to the town.

So what was school like here? Tiny. Imperfect. Close-knit. The kind of place where everyone knew your business but also where the whole island turned up to cheer you on.

Let's Go Lakers!

Sports on Mackinac were different. The school was K–12, all under one roof, which meant seniors and first graders shared hallways, some of the same teachers, and the playground. When it came to athletics, there weren't many kids to draw from, so rosters were thin. Everyone had to pitch in.

Some kids played everything. Soccer and volleyball in the fall, basketball in the winter, and then cross country or golf in the spring.

It made for some chaotic weekends. When we played against Beaver Island, the kids would fly there on chartered planes. Some would play a game of soccer, dash off the field, change uniforms, then play volleyball in the gym. At night, they'd order pizza, sleep on mats on the gym floor, and wake up early to do it all again. Then they'd fly home, uniforms rumpled, eyes bleary.

That was island athletics. Scrappy, exhausting, and absolutely unforgettable.

Grace had her lane: volleyball. From eighth grade through her senior year, she lived for it. Practices in the tiny gym, games where the bleachers rattled under stomping feet, and the sense of being part of something bigger than herself. I went to as many games as I could, slipping onto the hard bleachers and cheering the team on with the rest of the crowd. I might have missed a few when the hotel kept me tied up, but when I was there, I was all in.

The thing about Mackinac sports was that it wasn't just the parents in the stands. The whole community came. Islanders and locals showed up in force, filling the little gym like it was the NBA finals. Neighbors, grandparents, servers from the restaurants downtown, ferry crew on their night off. Everyone showed up to support the Lakers.

Winter was basketball season, and that's when the gym felt most alive. There were no Friday night football lights on Mackinac Island. Instead, we gathered under the fluorescent glare of the school gym, bundled coats tossed on the bleachers, the squeak of sneakers echoing off the walls. The elementary school cheer squad was always the highlight. Sweet little kids in matching outfits waving pom-poms, shouting their cheers with more enthusiasm than rhythm. The crowd loved them.

The opponents were always the same handful of small schools: Hannahville, Beaver Island, Maplewood, Grand Marais. Familiar gyms, familiar faces, the same cheers echoing across different bleachers. The Lakers didn't always win, but the community didn't care. The cheers were just as loud for a scrappy loss as they were for a blowout win. It was about the pride of showing up, of playing hard, of carrying the island's name across the water and back home again.

On Mackinac, sports weren't just something kids did after school. They were the heartbeat of the community, the glue that held the island together through long winters and shortened days. When the Lakers took the court, everyone was there.

How Does Everything Get Here?

On Mackinac, the ferries weren't just transportation. They were the island's heartbeat. They dictated everything. Miss the boat and you were stranded. Catch the last one and you were lucky.

I learned to line up on the commuter side of the dock, where Islanders and residents queued first, offering choice seats. The process never changed. Cars unloaded onto luggage carts, carts onto the ferry, then dispatched for drayage at the island dock. To tourists, it looked like chaos. To us, it was choreography.

For my guests, the ferry signaled the beginning of their Stonecliffe stay. On the mainland, their bags were tagged, marking their beginning origin and island destination. On the island, they rolled off the boat and began the journey to the hotel. Guests travelled by shuttle until 6:00 p.m., or by bicycle. Late arrivals sometimes required our porters to bike the luggage up the hill, and two miles to the hotel. It wasn't always calf-friendly, but the system worked.

Grace never loved the ferries. She preferred to fly. But she'd carve out her own quiet, occasionally catching a nap.

In the summer, Wednesdays were my day off, I'd head off-island for a grocery run. I'd load empty totes onto the shuttle and bike downtown, always stopping for coffee at Lucky Bean. Then I'd park my bike and join the shorter line reserved for seasonal or resident passes. I always sat in the same spot on the ferry, with just enough room to stretch out my legs and steal a twenty-minute nap before we docked, or to catch up on a good book.

On the mainland, my car was always waiting. The ferry company ran a valet system, the best perk of my island life. Even in winter, my car was stored inside, warmed up and ready by the time I arrived.

If I drove, it was usually to Cheboygan to shop at Walmart. While I shopped, Cooper got groomed at a mobile van in the parking lot. I'd pick him up before heading back to the boat, where I had to unload my groceries onto a luggage cart. They'd be wheeled onto the ferry alongside suitcases, bags of mulch, and everyone else's groceries. Back on the ferry, I'd take my usual seat, grab another twenty-minute nap, and then start the return leg. Then I'd pedal up the hill and wait for the horses to bring my groceries. Once, that meant waiting until the next day. Finally, I'd unpack everything, only to realize I'd forgotten to buy peanut butter.

The ferries carried everything. Guests, horses, groceries, luggage, even appliances. They were lifelines. Still, things had a way of disappearing in transit.

Once, we sent my stackable washer and dryer over to the mainland for repair. Horses hauled it to the dock, the ferry carried it to the mainland, a company picked it up, drove it to their shop, fixed it, and returned it to the dock. But then, it simply vanished. Gone, like it had slipped off the edge of the map. Nobody could explain it, and we never saw it again. Imagine that insurance claim. They had so many questions.

Storms tested even the routine crossings. I once rode through sideways rain, thunder rolling overhead, the ferry rocking hard enough to churn my stomach. But there was no turning back. On Mackinac, you crossed when you had to.

In winter, there was only one ferry, the Huron. It was smaller, sturdier, and built for ice. Island residents planned their lives around its schedule. Groceries, doctor's visits and hardware runs, all squeezed into its crossings. If the Huron didn't go, nobody went. And when it finally did nose through the ice into the harbor, it felt less like transportation and more like a lifeline.

By spring, the rhythm changed. We watched for the end of the winter schedule, hungering for flexibility. When the spring timetable arrived, the docks came alive. And by May, tourists reappeared, signaling once again that we had survived another Mackinac Island winter.

The Package Shuffle

To this day, I couldn't tell you what my actual employee housing address was in Oakwood Condos. I only knew: Oakwood, first apartment on the bottom left. My driver's license listed 8593 Cudahy Circle, the Mansion's address, because I needed to write *something* on the form. In reality, like everyone else, I had a P.O. box. The postmaster knew us all by name, and our box numbers by heart. That number felt as personal as any street address.

Nothing on Mackinac Island ever arrived when expected. Phone alerts that said "delivered" were just the beginning of a package's journey. It might land in St. Ignace, get signed for, get wrapped to a luggage cart, and be pushed onto the ferry for its ride across the

Straits. Once on the island, it got unloaded before passengers could even disembark, then sorted into its next chapter. Sometimes a hotel porter, sometimes the UPS gal, sometimes the Mackinac Island Service Company. They would load the packages and freight onto drays, which are horse-pulled flatbed carriages. With so many hands involved, it was astounding anything ever showed up at all.

UPS was actually the good kind of delivery. Those packages came by dray, right to your front door. Which we liked, because it saved us a trip all the way downtown. In winter, we didn't want to risk the horses trying to maneuver the downhill, unplowed, and often icy circle driveway to where I lived. Drivers would drop everything at the Summer House instead. It became normal for me to text Grace, "Swing by the Summer House after school and grab whatever showed up." That was our version of a front-porch drop-off.

Sometimes it ran in circles. One afternoon, I hopped on my snowmobile and went downtown to pick up a package from the Post Office. I hauled it all the way back to Stonecliffe in a utility trailer. The package was too heavy for me to carry down to my apartment from there, so I left it next to my snowmobile with the intention of returning with a sled, the kind kids play on hills with. By the time I made it back, the package was gone. A dray driver had picked it up, assuming it was outgoing, and delivered it right back downtown. My efficient round trip to the post office became a comedy routine.

The stakes could be serious too. Like the year I realized Grace's passport would expire while we were planning to be in Europe. That's not a little problem. That's a nightmare. I had to order an expedited passport and wait it out on the island while the whole machine worked its magic. It was a nerve-wracking few days, but by some miracle, the passport found its way into my hands on time.

Other times, the stories were just funny. Like the rug I ordered from Wayfair. The "delivered" notification really meant it had landed in St. Ignace and still had a ferry ride and a dray haul to go. Usually "delivered" meant you were still a day away from seeing your package. Sometimes you got lucky, sometimes not. A week passed. No rug. Records showed it to be delivered. Wayfair, bless them, sent a replacement without question. Then spring arrived, and with it the answer to the mystery. The original rug surfaced, having been misdelivered to a neighbor, then covered with snow for the rest of the winter. I ended up with two rugs and one more island delivery story to tell.

Lost guest luggage was its own brand of chaos. A groom once turned up furious, certain his suit had vanished. He described it as wrapped in a white trash bag. Hotels, ferry workers, porters, even businesses on the mainland were all on the lookout for a white-trash-bag-covered suit. We connected him with the only suit seller on the island, got him looking spiffy, and tried to calm him down. He was livid. Days later, he called to apologize. Turns out, he'd left the suit on his bed at home.

On Mackinac Island, "delivered" never meant delivered. It meant: stay tuned.

Life on Two Wheels

Our bikes were more than transportation. They were our lifelines to town. Every errand, every grocery run, every late-night dash for supplies depended on two wheels. If you wanted to get anywhere, the ferry dock, Doud's Market or the post office, you pedaled. On Mackinac, your bike was freedom. Without it, you were stranded. With it, the island opened up.

Every spring, the city lined up the stray bikes like a police lineup. Cruisers, clunkers, unclaimed and impounded. They had been parked where they shouldn't be, or left behind at the end of the season when their riders vanished with the last ferry. Every year, there was a bike auction, and seasonal workers could buy a bike instead of dragging theirs across on the ferry. It was practical and a little hilarious watching people shopping for a bike from last year's lost-and-found herd, testing squeaky brakes and crooked wheels, hoping the bike they'd chosen might survive another summer.

My first year, I was told to get rid of all the old Stonecliffe bikes, and so I did. We ordered about fifty new ones to use with our rotating licenses. They arrived in boxes, and someone had to put every last one together. Not me, thankfully. But I watched the process drag on, frame after frame, wheel after wheel. At the time, I thought new bikes would solve everything. By midsummer, I realized how useful it would have been to keep a few of those old beaters around for staff.

On Mackinac Island, bikes weren't stolen so much as relocated. Mine "wandered" more than once. In fact, it went missing three times that I can remember. Once, found at the Pink Pony, once at the Gatehouse, and once in the bushes near the Grand. Each recovery was equal parts relief and annoyance. After that, I finally gave in and started using a lock.

Bike baskets were a necessity on the island. Mine was huge, probably two feet by one, and could fit everything: my purse, packages, even the dog. It made the bike less sleek but far more useful. On Mackinac, a basket wasn't just an accessory, but a necessity, and part of our daily lives.

Another island lesson: always have bike fenders. Without them, whatever muck, mud, or horse-related mess you happen to ride through gets launched straight into the air and lands in a perfect stripe up the center of your back. You could always spot the tourists who brought their bikes from home.

Sometimes, randomly, we'd find our hotel rental bikes abandoned downtown. The porters had their own system for getting them back up the hill. They'd literally hoist the found bike onto the basket of a bright yellow porter bike and pedal it back up the hill to Stonecliffe. A porter on a bike, carrying a bike, wobbling uphill and somehow making it all the way. It was ridiculous. It was impressive. It was Mackinac.

I biked through every kind of weather, but the thunderstorms tested me most. Rain hit hard enough to sting, puddles grabbed at my pedals, and everything in my bike basket drenched. Lightning split the sky and still I kept pedaling, soaked through, because there was no other way home.

The time between winter and spring is a season itself. You can't safely get around on snowmobiles or bikes. The roads turn into a patchwork of bare concrete and stubborn snow, with puddles in between. It isn't pretty, but you take the good with the bad in exchange for living in this magical place.

And then there was the big hill beside the Grand Hotel. This hill carries its own legend. The rule was simple.

Pedal as far as the little post in the ground, the Weenie Post. If you didn't make it that far, it was open season, and kids could gleefully call you a weenie. The memory of burning lungs is strong.

One year, two girls rented a tandem bike, a bike with two seats and two sets of pedals, downtown and biked all the way up to Stonecliffe. They parked it in our rental line by mistake, and our brand-new house porter didn't know any better. He promptly rented it out to one of our guests. By the time the girls finished eating, their tandem bike was gone. We did what we always did in those situations. We improvised. We sent them back downtown on one of our tandems and waited for theirs to make its way home. Eventually, all the bikes found their way back to the right racks.

We learned not to take it personally. Lock what you love, ride what you can, and if your bike goes missing, start with the bushes and the bars. On an island without cars, bikes were currency, transportation, and sometimes communal property. Bikes didn't vanish. They just went on adventures without you.

Horse Power

On Mackinac Island, nothing simply appears. Everything begins with the ferry. Even a Sysco truck rolled onto a boat, riding the Straits with its cargo of restaurant food and supplies. At the dock, the doors swung open and the unloading began.

From there, it's all horses. Shuttle and taxi teams carry guests and luggage up the hill, hour by hour. Dray horses haul the freight, food, packages, kegs and garbage.

Then there were the two-footers, the trash drays. The Mackinac Island Service Company would drop one off at the hotel, an open wagon waiting to be filled. The island equivalent of mainlanders ordering a garbage dumpster for home improvement projects. We built walls inside with whatever scraps we had so we could stack in as much waste as possible. When it was full, a call to the Service Company brought a team to haul it away.

All that manure had a destination, too. Street sweepers and carts collected it through the day, and wagons hauled it to the city's composting site. There, it was piled with food scraps and yard waste, and turned over until it became rich topsoil. That soil found its way back into island gardens and landscaping, proof that even the mess under a horse's hooves had a purpose.

Not all horses did the same work. The dray horses were the biggest and strongest, hauling freight and garbage. The Grand Hotel had their own elegant teams, pulling carriages full of guests dressed up for dinner. Then there were saddle horses for trail rides, taxi horses moving visitors through town, and the three-horse teams that powered the island's famous Carriage Tours.

Guests often asked if the horses were overworked. They weren't. A shuttle team would head out for a morning shift, work a few hours, then return to the barn for hay and water while a fresh team came out for the afternoon. Along the way, water troughs waited at corners, so horses had more breaks, and more to drink, than most of us working alongside them.

It wasn't glamorous, but it worked. Supplies crossed the water and got hauled to their destinations, and unloaded, piece by piece. Life moved to the steady sound of hooves on pavement. Unhurried, reliable and deliberate.

What Is It Like to Work Here?

Not every day at Stonecliffe was perfect. Far from it. But when I look back, it's the bright ones I find myself telling stories about.

This was a good day at Stonecliffe:

I'd wake to the sound of horse hooves on the pavement and birdsong outside my window. After a quiet cup of coffee and a brisk dog walk, I headed in to work.

By eleven, I was on the front porch, helping with luggage if needed and seeing the shuttle off. I chatted with the porters and front desk manager about departures, who was working, what needed to be done. I made small talk with guests on the porch. Everyone seemed happy and curious.

The porch itself was its own kind of stage. In the morning, coffee cups clinked as people planned their day.

Every morning, I reviewed the arrival report so I'd know who to expect. If a familiar family was coming back, or if a VIP had booked, I sometimes arranged for a welcome amenity to be waiting in their room with a handwritten note.

I stopped by the front desk, then cut through the bar and out to the Portico. That view, water shimmering, the bridge in the distance, always gave me pause.

In the kitchen, I said my good mornings and snagged a leftover breakfast sausage. The chef was already prepping for the evening meal, and the air smelled warm and comforting.

Out back, I grabbed some of the leftover flowers from last night's wedding and carried a bouquet to my office. They brightened the whole room and gave the flowers a second life.

Housekeeping ran steady, everyone showed up, rooms were covered, no big complaints. Just smiles and small jokes as carts rolled down the halls.

Maintenance stayed busy with the usual, tightening up a bike chain, fixing a leaky faucet, nothing urgent. It was the kind of work that made the whole place run, everything ticking exactly as it should.

The day moved easily. Bills got paid, mail sorted, phone calls answered. I dropped in with the sales manager and the front office manager, trading laughter and quick stories before heading back to my office.

The bar opened at four, the restaurant at five. I always popped in to say hello. The bartenders would be polishing glasses and stocking wine, and the servers would be lining up silverware. The calm before the guests arrived.

The chef set out a sample for the staff, and I tasted whatever had been plated. Every bite felt like a treat.

If there was a wedding that night, I'd often step in for dinner service if needed, or I'd cover the bar. Wedding toasts made everyone cry, the DJ controlled the flow, and plates went out smoothly. It was a fun kind of frenzy.

When everything went as it should, you could feel it in the air. Guests thought it was effortless, as if Stonecliffe simply ran itself. But from my vantage point, I knew it was housekeeping, servers, bartenders, maintenance, front desk, kitchen, and porters all working in sync. When that orchestra played in harmony, the result was a perfect stay.

As the sun sank, I stepped onto the Portico and watched the sky turn gold and pink, the water catching every color. Then I locked my office door and took a slow walk home, savoring the sunset, the Mackinac Bridge, and the crickets chirping off in the distance.

That was a good day. The kind I'll always be nostalgic for.

Employee Housing

One of the questions I got asked often was, "Where do all your employees live?" There were late ferries in peak season, and some downtown businesses housed staff on the mainland. But for us at Stonecliffe, with the hotel perched far from the docks, commuting didn't make sense. So the answer was simple. We housed them right on the island.

The biggest hub was a building we called Olde Barn. On the outside it looked like a normal apartment building. Inside, well, let's just say it had personality. One bathroom had two toilets sitting side by side, no stall walls, no dividers. Just two porcelain thrones in a row, as if someone thought bathroom time should be a social event. Nobody could explain it, and we eventually stopped trying. Quirks like that just came with the territory.

Most rooms were basic, with twin beds, a dresser, and a shared bathroom down the hall. People decorated however they could. They'd string Christmas lights and hang posters. There always ended up being mismatched chairs, salvaged from town curbs. By July, housing never looked the way it had in May. Bike racks overflowed, music drifted from open doors, and the halls were busy at all hours as shifts started and ended.

By midsummer, housing had a life of its own. New staff arrived with fresh enthusiasm in May, a few homesick faces slipped away by June, and by July everyone left had settled into the routine. Meals came out of the shared kitchens. Sometimes pasta, sometimes something new and unfamiliar brought by staff from across the world. Housing felt like a little village, with its own inside jokes, favorite spots, and unspoken rules.

Five employees got to stay right in the basement of the Mansion. Most considered themselves lucky; close to the kitchens, laundry, even the timeclock, which sat outside their door. They could roll out of bed and be at work in under a minute. But that convenience was also the curse. When your bedroom was twenty steps from work, you didn't really get a day off. Those folks had to head out hiking or biking just to feel like they'd escaped the job.

Tulecki was a little four-unit house at the Four Corners. That was manager housing, a definite step up from dorm life. Private studios with real, albeit small, kitchenettes. Those spots were coveted, and once someone landed one, they weren't giving it up until the last ferry of the season.

I was always honest when people asked about housing. Usually I'd say, "It's not glamorous, but it's how the island works." And it was. Without housing, there would've been no cooks, no housekeepers, no porters. No hotel at all.

It wasn't perfect, but it was necessary. And in its own quirky way, housing became part of the Mackinac Island adventure.

Do You Have a Car?

It was one of the first things people asked when they learned I lived on Mackinac Island year-round. The follow-up came just as easily. “Where do you park?”

I had the best answer possible. Star Line Ferry, now operating under new management as Arnold Transit Company, gave me free valet parking every year in exchange for using them as our main ferry partner. Deal.

Arriving was effortless. I’d pull up, unload my car, and hand over my keys. They’d whisk my car away to… somewhere. A garage, a lot? I never really knew.

Once, a friend told me they'd been shuttled in my car because it was "on the way." Apparently, my car moonlighted as a courtesy van.

If I was leaving the island, I'd call the ferry company and let them know which boat I'd be on. I'd bike the two miles, ride the ferry, and when we got there, my car would be waiting, heat running if it was winter. Spoiled, I know. Most people had to pay for parking and then trudge or shuttle out to find their cars. For me, valet the best perk of my island life.

Leaving the island always turned into a checklist. Haircut, oil change, dentist, groceries, hardware store. Every errand packed into one day on the mainland. Driving didn't feel strange. It felt efficient. What *did* feel strange was spotting familiar faces from the island behind the wheel. Someone you only ever saw on a bike or in a carriage suddenly waving from a car window. It always caught me off guard, like when you were a kid and see your third-grade teacher at the grocery store.

In the deep of winter, when the ferry wasn't running due to ice, we'd have to fly over. That meant leaving my car parked at the Mackinac County Airport in St. Ignace for weeks, sometimes months. Coming back was a ritual. Shovel it out from the latest Upper Peninsula snow storm, then tackle the walls left by the plows. I've spent literal hours digging myself free.

I'd chip away at the ice, shovel a path to the door, and let the engine run while I finished the job. There was something satisfying about freeing the car myself. A small victory in the midst of a long winter.

People always imagined island living as simple and slow. They didn't picture me waist-deep in snow, coaxing my frozen car to life. But that's Mackinac for you. Equal parts postcard and practicality.

Is This Place Haunted?

Guests arrive with the question already formed, “Is this place haunted?” The conversation followed a familiar pattern. Some leaned in, hoping to hear stories about ghosts, while others laughed it off.

Some swear Candlelight is the room with activity, while others point a firm finger at Maplewood.

One man insisted a ghost borrowed his razor, proof that a ghost exists. Others reported flickering lights. Every once in a while, someone got spooked enough to move rooms.

I let my daughter and a friend sleep in the Mansion’s Candlelight Room one quiet fall night after the hotel had closed for the season. Teenagers make anything into a dare. They declared the remote control "possessed" when it kept misbehaving, but nothing else happened. They woke up, rolled their eyes, and came home for pancakes.

I've done my share of waiting for something to happen. In winter I've sat in that same bridge-facing room. I'll admit it did feel a little creepy. It reminded me of the movie "The Shining." But I didn't see or feel anything amiss.

Still, there were places in the Mansion that made my shoulders rise a notch. The closet under the grand stairwell that carries guests from the lobby to the second floor is nothing but a storage pocket where we stored bat nets, luggage tags and island brochures. But it always creeped me out. I never lingered.

The staff kept the stories alive. Year after year, Candlelight took the spotlight in their retellings. One season, a front desk associate even declared the ghost had a name: Rachel. I don't know if that stuck, or how many guests have since retold the story. That is how lore is made. Passed by word of mouth, season by season.

The island adds its own chorus. On the front porch, guests asked not just about Stonecliffe but about other Mackinac rumors. Harvey at Mission Point, the soldier at Fort Mackinac, the crooked Catholic steeple, even the occasional whisper about footsteps where there shouldn't be any. Taxi drivers told stories about a screaming figure near the stone gates and how it startled them on late-night runs.

Some believed. Some didn't.

When my daughter was young, we joined the "Haunts of Mackinac" ghost walk. It was technically for adults and older kids, but we got special permission. We learned about the island's spirit map, forts and theaters and tucked-away corners. At Mission Point they handed out little ghost trackers that lit up if a presence was nearby. Hers lit up, and she bolted toward me on instinct, half-laughing, the way kids do when they're scared and thrilled at the same time. Was it a battery quirk? Probably. Did it matter? Not at all.

If there are spirits at Stonecliffe, I like to think they're the friendly kind. A servant, proud of her duties. If she walks at night, I imagine she's checking on things. Turning down a bedspread, smoothing a curtain so the view is just so.

So, when guests asked, as they always did, "Is this place haunted?" I passed the question back to them. "What do you think?"

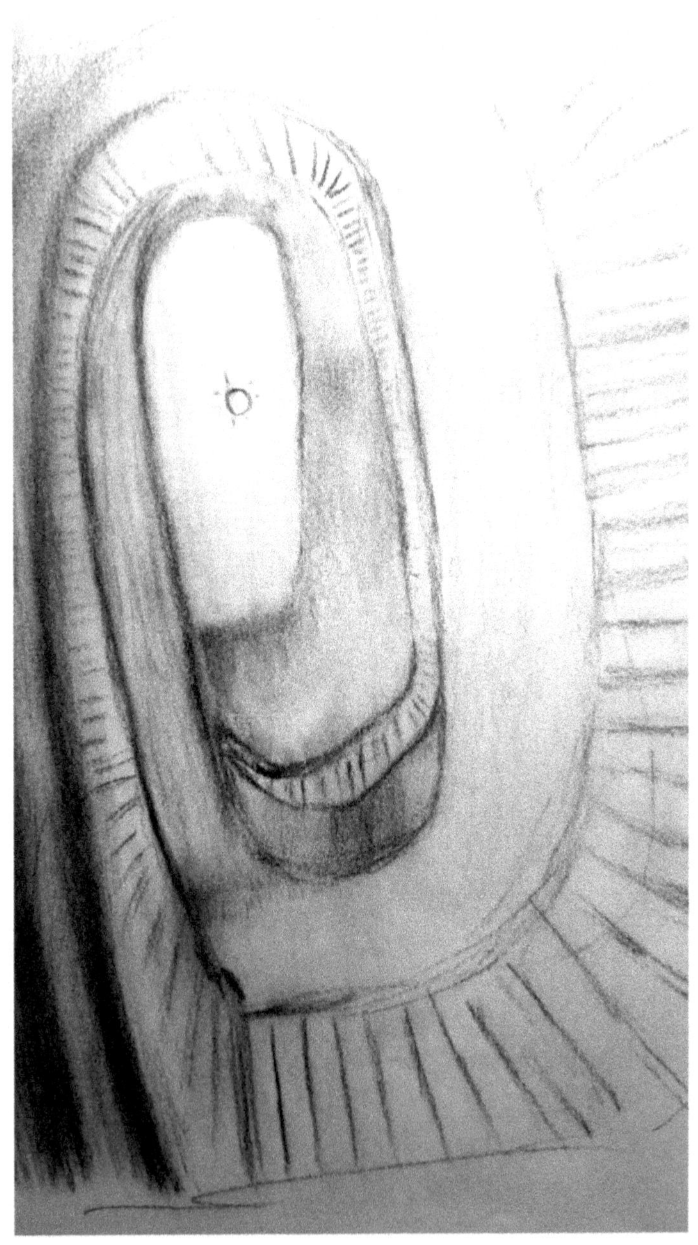

What Is Your Favorite Season Up Here?

Without doubt, fall on Mackinac Island was my favorite season. The Tuesday after Labor Day felt like someone flipped a switch, and the whole island finally calmed down. The ferries still ran, but fewer. The streets emptied. Even the horses seemed to walk slower, their hooves clicking against pavement littered with leaves. The air smelled different. Earthy, a little damp with morning dew, edged with that sharp lake breeze that warned winter was coming. Mornings carried a chill now, the kind that made you pull on a sweater before heading outside.

Maybe it felt so peaceful because of what came right before. The island calls it Angry August. By then, staff were stretched thin, exhausted and reckless, sneaking drinks on the job or skipping shifts altogether. Everyone was running hot. Tempers were short, patience was gone. Some staff didn't last the whole season for a variety of reasons. But the ones who stayed? Those were my people. If they made it through August, they were almost always in it until the end.

But in September, the kids were back in school, fall weddings began, and suddenly I found myself surrounded by silence instead of constant noise. The angry tide rolled back, leaving behind the people who were still standing. Staff committed to seeing the season through, guests who came not to conquer the island, but to savor it. Even the employees began to breathe differently.

Then came the color. The maples lit up first, followed by the oaks, until the island was every shade of gold and crimson. Even my short walk to work turned into something worth pausing for. The air felt clearer somehow, the lake sharper, like the whole island had taken a deep breath and decided to show off before winter came.

The pace shifted. We decorated the Mansion with pumpkins, mums, and scarecrows. The landscaping company came through with their blowers, pushing piles of leaves into the woods until the grass was clear again. There was time to walk downtown for a coffee or a drink, time to stand on the porch at dusk and notice the streets empty out at night. Most of the day-trippers were gone and in their place was quiet, broken only by the clip-clop of horse hooves, or the rustle of leaves in the wind.

For me, fall was always marked by the fireplace in my housing. I didn't burn it in summer, but in September, it came back to life. Logs stacked, flames steady, the apartment carrying that faint wood smoke scent that meant the season had changed.

Best of all was my front porch. Coffee in hand, I sat wrapped in a blanket in an Adirondack chair overlooking the Straits, sipping from the mug as the island slowed down around me. From there I could watch the water deepen into a darker blue and the trees flare with color. I could hear only the wind, the lake, and the occasional clip clop from horses.

In fall, Mackinac gave us permission to exhale.

Mackoween

One of the things I loved most about fall on Mackinac was the island's annual Halloween festivities. My first year on the island, I had no idea how legendary they really were. The hotel had closed for the season, which meant no guests, no arrivals, no staffing puzzles to solve. Friends invited me downtown that weekend, and I could not believe what I saw. Every bar was packed wall to wall with elaborate costumes and group themes people had clearly spent all year planning. It remains, to this day, the best Halloween party I have ever experienced.

Eventually, the weekend became my own tradition, what I affectionately called Mackoween. Every year, a group of friends would ferry over for the weekend and stay at the closed hotel while I played unofficial innkeeper. Friday nights meant bowls of homemade chili around the chiminea while cold lake air settled over the island, or gatherings in the mansion's bar, decorated with Halloween festiveness. One year we went on a hayride. Another year, we took a private carriage tour led by an island legend.

Every year brought a different costume theme. We were zombies, Waldos, 80's girls, gnomes, superheroes, scarecrows, and even street signs.

The bike ride around the island became one of the defining traditions of the weekend. Sometimes we rode in costume, stopping at every mile marker for photos. Once, at Mile Marker 5, someone performed the Worm right there in the middle of M-185.

Of all the Halloween weekends, the scarecrow year stands out the most because my sisters and mom were there. Earlier that day, my big sister had run the Great Turtle Half Marathon, while the rest of us dressed as cowgirls for the bike ride around the island. That night, everybody transformed into scarecrows while I dressed as the crow. We spent the evening weaving through packed bars, dancing, taking pictures, and trying not to lose each other in the crowds. Around eleven o'clock, a massive thunderstorm rolled over the island, and in the middle of the chaos, everybody got separated downtown.

Eventually, sometime after midnight, I gave up trying to find everyone and started the long bike ride uphill alone in the storm. My crow costume was soaked. Black feathers hung limp against my arms, my wings flapping wildly behind me while thunder cracked overhead. The eyes of my mask had fogged with rain, and I pedaled uphill half laughing and half miserable through one of the wildest storms I can remember on Mackinac.

The next morning, everybody showed up for breakfast in my apartment with their own ridiculous story. One person accidentally ended up at the wrong apartment building and wandered for an hour in the storm before finally finding SummerHouse. Another unknowingly pushed her bike up Turkey Hill instead of Grand Hill, quickly learning there was a vast difference between the two. One friend recovered a lost wallet, phone, and AirPods by retracing his route back to town the next morning.

As much as I loved fall most of all, every season on Mackinac had its own kind of magic. Spring and early summer brought the Lilac Festival, purple everywhere, and the sweet scent of lilacs drifting through the streets. Summer belonged to sunset, long glowing evenings where the sky exploded into color over the water and everybody seemed to pause for a moment just to watch. One night, I even saw a rainbow, a hummingbird, and a brilliant sunset all at the same time, which felt almost impossibly beautiful.

Winter had its hold on me too. Fresh snow gathered on the tree branches until the woods became tunnels of white, so quiet and beautiful they hardly felt real. But in the end, fall always won me over. The cool air, changing leaves, bike rides, Halloween weekends, and that sweet realization that we could finally relax and unwind for a few months out of guests' view. There was just something about fall on Mackinac that felt magical to me.

Epilogue

I spent eight years on Mackinac Island, long enough to know it by heart. The ferries set the pace, the horses kept the island moving, and the bridge marked the horizon. Every season, new guests arrived with the same questions, and I never tired of answering them. “Do you do weddings?” “How do you get groceries?” “Where do the employees live?” “Is this place haunted?” I must have told those stories a thousand times, and somehow, they never grew old.

Some days were harder than others, but the island was always the backdrop that held everything together. I watched summers stretch into fall, winters bite down, and spring bring the island back to life again. Staff came and went, managers changed, but Mackinac remained. Ferry horns across the Straits, bike bells on the hill, horses lining the streets, and sunsets catching on the water.

That was the gift of the job. Guests thought they were asking small questions, but they were really asking about a way of life. About rhythm and routine, weather and work, and what it means to build a world without cars or shortcuts, where improvisation was part of everyday life.

I returned to Mackinac Island in 2025 for the first time since leaving in 2020. I went to visit a dear friend and pay my respects at her husband's grave. While I was there, I found myself walking through the rain all the way back up to Stonecliffe. I wanted to see it again.

The new Stonecliffe is beautiful. Really beautiful. The mansion has been lovingly restored, the grounds expanded, and new gathering spaces now overlook the water where guests sit watching the sunset. There are cottages tucked into the lawn, fire pits glowing at dusk, and a wedding pavilion that would have saved us countless discussions about tent flaps and weather forecasts back in the day.

Walking through the front doors again felt strangely familiar and completely different at the same time. I loved it, but it was a different kind of love. It is possible to love the same thing in two ways. I loved the old Stonecliffe very much, but I found myself loving the new version too. They did a really good job, exactly what you would expect with the kind of investment they put into it.

Life has moved on in other ways too. My daughter grew up on that island and has since earned her commercial pilot license, and is now working for EAA in Oshkosh, Wisconsin, which somehow feels fitting. Mackinac opened doors neither of us could have imagined at the time, and for that we are grateful.

I've left Mackinac Island now, but it's still in me. The sound of hooves, the smell of lilacs, the sight of the bridge stretched across the water. Those things stay.

How could they not?

www.ingramcontent.com/pod-product-compliance
Lightning Source LLC
LaVergne TN
LVHW021159160826
845679LV00024B/2170

* 9 7 9 8 9 9 4 8 9 1 8 1 0 *